5/02

ACROBATICS is dedicated to these lovely people:

Kent Austin, an excellent photographer;

Rick Takahashi, a skillful cartoonist;

Sharon Waag, my talented sketch artist;

Dotty Stewart McGill, a beautiful and gifted dancing school director and teacher, who through the years has shared so much with so many;

Porter R. and John A. McCandless, my father and uncle, self-taught acrobats, who as young men chose the college education route instead of traveling with the Barnum and Bailey Circus;

Rex (12), Dee (10), and Dana Polley (9), our three acrobats who are a constant challenge and inspiration;

Janet Muller, my sister, a national judge and gymnastics coach at Kent State University, Boardman Branch.

Maxine Polley

acrobatics

photographs by Kent Austin
cartoons by Rick Takahashi

PRENTICE-HALL, INC.
Englewood Cliffs, New Jersey

To my darling daughter
Annette

Interior Design by Dawn L. Stanley

Photographs on pages 20, 22, 28, 42, and 54 by Mick Webster.

Copyright © 1981 by Maxine Polley

1 2 3 4 5 6 7 8 9 10

Prentice-Hall International, Inc., London
Prentice-Hall of Australia, Pty. Ltd., North Sydney
Prentice-Hall of Canada, Ltd., Toronto
Prentice-Hall of India Private Ltd., New Delhi
Prentice-Hall of Japan, Inc., Tokyo
Prentice-Hall of Southeast Asia Pte. Ltd., Singapore
Whitehall Books Limited, Wellington, New Zealand

Library of Congress Cataloging in Publication Data
Polley, Maxine. Acrobatics.
Includes index.
SUMMARY: An introduction to the fundamentals of
acrobatics, stressing techniques, form, and safety.
1. Acrobats and acrobatism—Juvenile literature.
[1. Acrobats and acrobatics] I. Austin, Kent. II. Title.
GV551.P6 796.4'7   80-10422 ISBN 0-13-003079-1

iv

contents

Introduction
viii

rolls 1

5

splits, stands, walks 55

6

springs 79

introduction

M OVEMENT and the child are natural companions. Youngsters have native curiosity and motivation for movement with seemingly boundless energy, all qualities essential for outstanding acrobats.

More and more acrobatic skills are appearing in Elementary Physical Education programs. Winning Floor Exercise routines at the Secondary level, on TV and in the Olympics, feature acrobatic maneuvers. With such fantastic growth in the last ten years, intermediate skills are now considered basic, and basics are fundamental.

Even Olympic champions begin with basics. Olga Korbut, the pony-tailed "little sprite" on the Russian team, delighted thousands of spectators while touring America. At age nine, Olga was a better athlete than many boys her age. Besides enjoying sports, she liked to play with dolls and collect stuffed animals. For her, "it was so painful being so small." Performing a new skill correctly made her feel nine feet tall. She enjoyed winning! At age twelve she entered a major contest. When fifteen, Olga won the gold medal. When still a school girl, she became an Olympic champion.

What makes a champion? Olympic hopefuls start acrobatics when very young and work hard at what they love to do best. They must always follow safety procedures: work on the carpet or grass, always practice with others, warm up properly by stretching the muscles, begin with basics, and always learn the skill well before moving on progressively. Even champions follow their teacher's advice as they learn new tricks for routines.

ACROBATICS begins each section with the easiest skills. How many of these skills have you seen before? Which ones have you already done in Physical Education class? Do you see some new ones you would like to learn? Talk to your Physical Education teacher about them. He/she can help you have fun!

X

Chapter 1

rolls

THE ROLL is thought to be the most fundamental acrobatic or tumbling skill. In the tuck body position, the legs are bent or flexed next to the chest so the acrobat can roll like a ball. For rolls in pike position, the legs remain straight or extended while the acrobat bends at the hips to roll. As the hips touch the mat, the legs flex to stand. The many attractive roll variations provide challenge for youngsters and add beauty to floor exercise routines.

As your skills mature, you can transfer what you learn on the mats to gymnastic equipment. For example, the forward and backward rolls done on the floor can also be done on the 4-inch-wide balance beam.

Learning to roll properly is also a safety measure. When trying new stunts, the acrobat often overbalances, then must roll out to keep from getting hurt. A good rule to remember is when you make a mistake, roll for safety.

tuck forward roll walk-out

Standing with feet together, bend the legs, reach forward and place the hands on the mat, shoulder width apart. Push on the hands, tuck the head bringing the chin downward, and put the back of the head on the mat. At the same time, lift the hips. Roll to stand on the forward leg with arms extended over head. Spotter or helper: steady the upper arm and guide the tuck with the other hand on the back of the head.

pike forward roll
walk-out

With straight legs, reach forward and
place the hands on the mat. Tuck the head as you
bend the arms (don't relax), while lifting the hips.
Roll. Walk-out to stand.

tuck backward roll

From a squat position with the weight forward on the hands, push off, sit back (still with chin down), then <u>quickly</u> move the hands above the shoulders (palm up). Catching the body weight on the hands, <u>push</u> and roll. Land on the feet, legs flexed in squat position. With a walk-out separate the legs when pushing on the hands, and land on just one foot. Spotter: lift the hips as the child rolls.

straddle
backward roll

Standing with feet apart, <u>lean</u> forward,
extending the arms backward (fingers forward)
between the legs. Keeping the legs straight,
continue to <u>lean</u> forward as you sit down, catching
the weight on the hands. Quickly bring the hands
above the shoulders, push, <u>pull</u> the stomach in to
land with feet apart. Spotters: hold the upper arm.
Working on a crash pad is better still. The forward
straddle roll takes more momentum.

pike backward roll

With legs together <u>lean</u> forward, sit down
(legs straight), catching the weight on the hands
positioned beside the hips. While pulling in at the
waist, quickly place the hands just above the
shoulders and <u>push.</u> Extend the arms and stand. As
a lead-up skill, practice pushing off with the hands,
shifting the weight to the feet, stand then repeat.
Spotters: keep acrobat from sitting down too hard
by holding upper arm.

back pike roll lead-up

Sitting with one leg bent or flexed,
roll, landing on the foot of the bent leg. Touch the
other one back with knee outward.

dive rolls for height

After flexing (bending) the legs and arms,
arch the arms upward, pushing off with the feet
and lifting the hips. Catch the body weight on the
hands, then upper back, keeping the head tucked.
Roll and stand. Remember, as you add running
steps, be sure to use a two-foot take-off. It's fun to
dive over piled up cardboard boxes! Crashing
usually isn't too serious.

dive rolls for distance

As you push off with the feet, extend the arms forward. As the body comes downward, <u>catch</u> the weight on the hands, then upper back, <u>tucking</u> the head. Roll, then stand. First master diving over one cardboard box, then try several! Do not overestimate your ability.

handstand
forward roll

Kick to a handstand, one foot at a time.
Overbalance the legs to begin the roll. <u>Bend</u> or flex
the arms and <u>tuck</u> the head to roll, then stand.
Spotters: catch legs above the knee and let go only
after she starts to roll.

back extension

Begin with a pike backward roll.
Momentum will help you <u>push</u> up into a handstand.
<u>Pull</u> in at the waist, push off with the hands, flex
the legs as you land on both feet, or walk-out,
landing on one. Spotters: catch the legs above the
knees in a handstand.

THIS MAY HURT MY PRIDE!

EVERYTHING IS UPSIDE...
DOWN

fun series

Practice these combinations down the mat. They are great for demonstrations or exhibitions.

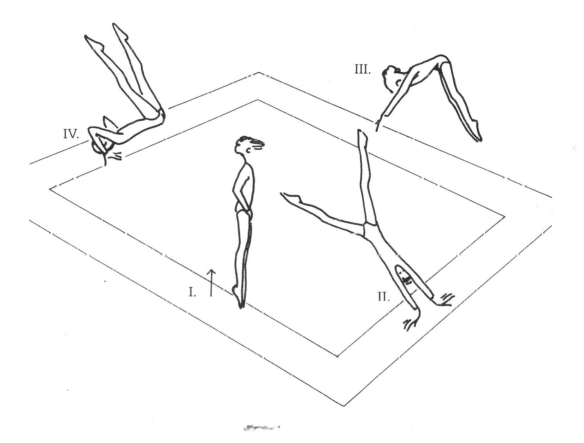

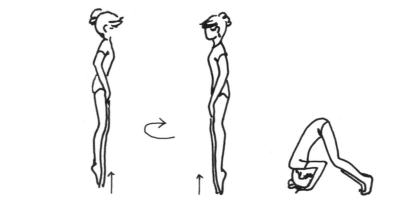

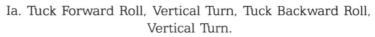

Ia. Tuck Forward Roll, Vertical Turn, Tuck Backward Roll, Vertical Turn.

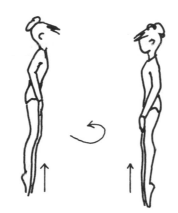

Ib. Pike Forward Roll, Vertical Turn, Pike
Backward Roll, Vertical Turn.

II. Cartwheel, One-Handed Cartwheel, Roundoff.

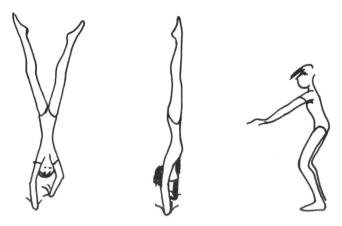

II. Continued, showing the Roundoff.

III. Handstand Forward Roll, Dive Roll for Height, Handstand
Forward Roll Walk-Out.

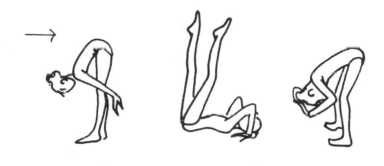

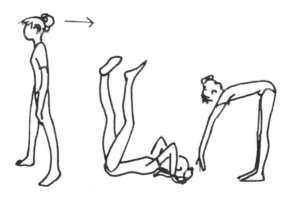

IV. Pike Backward Roll into Straddle position, Backward Straddle Roll, Back Straddle Roll ending in Pike position.

Chapter 2

wheels

W HEELS include Cartwheels and Roundoffs, plus their variations. The roundoff is an exciting trick! You are headed one direction, then all of a sudden you face the other. This is an especially important skill, because later on difficult skills are added to it. It must be straight and fast.

Practice cartwheels and roundoffs on both sides (face the other direction and lead with the other hand). This will help to develop muscles equally on both sides, thus preventing curvatures of the spine (crooked backbone).

beginner
cartwheel

Facing the side with feet apart, use a <u>four-count</u> placement (hand, hand, foot, foot) in an <u>even rhythm</u>. The legs don't have to be vertical, just as long as they get off the ground. Eye focus is on the mat. Spotter: face the acrobat's back, cross arms and lift her hips.

standard
cartwheel

Standing sideways with the feet apart and arms
up, use an <u>even four-count</u> placement of the
hands then feet, keeping legs and arms <u>straight</u>,
up toward the ceiling.

In the One Hand Cartwheel, place one hand out or
on the hip, <u>pulling in</u> more at the waist before
landing. For alternate cartwheels, do one facing
one direction, move the back foot forward, body
facing the other direction, and repeat the
cartwheel. This way you will exercise both sides
of the body. Spotter: same as for beginner
cartwheel.

alternate cartwheels

Execute one cartwheel, <u>step</u> forward
with the <u>back</u> foot and face the other side. Do
another cartwheel, thus exercising both sides of
the body.

NOW YOU SEE
MY FACE...

...NOW YOU
DON'T

roundoff

With eye focus front, begin like a
cartwheel. However, place the second hand <u>quicker</u>,
<u>closer</u> and <u>past</u> the midline on the mat. After the
one-foot take-off, the legs are apart. <u>Hit</u> the feet
together when the body is vertical, <u>turning</u> the hips
to face the direction you came from. <u>Pull in</u> at the
waist, <u>pushing</u> off with the hands. Spring upward
as you land, feet together. Practice on a line in
the gym.

cartwheel limber

Begin like a cartwheel, then bring
the legs <u>together</u> into a handstand. Go over as in a
limber (see description) and stand. What great <u>fun</u>
to change directions! Spotter: face acrobat on the
mat. With one hand on her back, assist her
coming up.

butterflies

Kids nine years old and up are doing butterflies, but maybe not as high and straight as thirteen-year-olds. A butterfly is a diagonal cartwheel done without the use of the hands. With the feet apart and leaning forward somewhat, start by swinging the arms horizontally in the opposite direction you plan to go (the wind-up). Now, swing the arms and head <u>downward</u>, toward the back of the lead leg, then <u>pull upward</u> elevating the body. <u>Push off</u> with the lead foot, swinging the other leg diagonally upward. <u>Pull in</u> at the waist to land on that leg. Isn't it fun to be in the air, even for a few moments!

Carol's arched
cartwheel special

This skill is much like four very arched
cartwheels in a circle, but without standing up
between each skill and rebounding or springing
from the feet. With the use of momentum, it
becomes fast, even spectacular.

aerial cartwheel

Aerial means without the use of the hands. The power comes from the <u>push-off</u> with the lead leg and the <u>downward</u>, then <u>upward</u> powerful pull with the arms. Correct <u>timing</u> is essential. A gymnastic belt held by spotters and the use of an incline (rubber-covered board) are helpful. The ankles are saved from injury, and success comes sooner.

Chapter 3

limbers

BESIDES being pretty to look at, the limber group members are excellent for strengthening and toning up the stomach (abdominal) muscles. There is nearly a complete circle of stretch. Even sit-ups don't stretch muscles that much. Limber variations, such as Inside Outs, exercise the upper back muscles. Limbers are much enjoyed by very young children. Their inchworm-like flexibility adds extra beauty to the skills. These overall body builders contribute to the current emphasis on health promotion.

rocker

First, do a bird's nest. While on the stomach push on the hands and arch back, touching the toes to the head. Next, rock on the stomach catching the weight on the hands.

"Do a bird's nest and Rock... WHO THOUGHT OF THIS CRAZY THING?"

crabwalk

From a position on the back, push up onto all fours. Keeping the fingers extended toward the shoulders, walk forward and back with hands <u>shoulder</u> width apart.

inside outs

Do a push-up back bend width-wise on the mat. Shift the weight to the feet, then reach one arm over while twisting the body. Bring the leg over. Now on all fours and facing the mat, shift then reach, ending in crab position as you began. Spotter: holding acrobat with both hands at the waist, back up as she moves toward you.

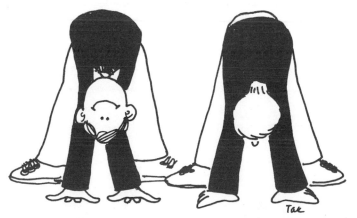

back bend

First, learn to come up from a bridge
or crab position. By yourself, <u>walk</u> in very close,
<u>lean forward</u> at the thighs, keeping the head <u>back</u>.
When mastered, learn to go down by yourself. <u>Lean
forward</u> at the thighs. With head <u>back</u>, <u>lead with
straight arms, catching</u> the weight on the hands.
Spotter: facing the acrobat, pull forward and
upward.

circle inside outs

Place the hands close and the feet
farther apart each time you face the mat on all
fours, making a circle.

forward chest rolls

Begin on your knees turning the face to one side, push on the hands in front of the shoulders, bending the legs. Roll over in arched position landing on the knees. When mastered, begin from a standing position, land standing. If very flexible, hold the ankles and do continuous rolls. Children with very limber backs love to do this trick. Have the teacher watch and lift at the waist if needed when doing it the first time.

cartwheel
inside outs

From a back bend, reach over and cartwheel.
As the foot lands, go into the inside out back bend
position. Repeat several times without standing
between skills in the circle.

front limber

Kick one leg up at a time into a vertical
handstand. Arch the back, keeping the head back
(towards the upper back). Flex the legs, landing
with the feet apart. Come up as from a back bend.
Spotter: to the side of the acrobat, assist with one
hand on her back.

tuck arabian limber

With the hands on the mat, flex or bend
the legs, then <u>lift</u> the hips over the head while
extending the legs vertically into a handstand. <u>Arch</u>
the back and keep the head <u>back</u>, coming up as
from a back bend.

One, two, three. Look at me. I passed beginners, I'm a winner

back limber

Do a back bend; however, push off with the feet just before the hands touch the mat. Pass the legs through a vertical handstand, landing with feet together. Some teach the back walkover beginning. Spotter: at the side, place one hand under the lead leg, the other on the lower back.

pike arabian limber

With the hands on the mat, bend the legs. Push off with the feet, extending your legs straight at a 90-degree angle from the hips. With hips leading over the head, pull legs to a vertical handstand. Continue as in a front limber. You may walk-out.

Chapter 4

walkovers

WALKOVERS and their many variations are among the most beautiful of acrobatic skills. Mechanically, the walkover begins and ends on one foot. The deeper the arch and the larger the side split position, the more attractive the picture. Practicing walkovers increases body flexibility and develops grace and balance.

front walkover

Use a one-foot kick-off into a handstand, keeping the legs in a side split. With the head back, arch the back, bend the lead leg to land. Bring the head and arms up last as you stand. Shift forward, extending the back leg. Spotter: to the side of the lead leg, place one hand on her back and the other under the thigh.

aeroplane
walkover

Begin as in a front walkover.

Tap the foot (last to leave the ground) just above the knee of the extended leg. Open into a side split handstand again, walkover out and stand.

scissor walkover

Kick up to a split handstand
<u>leading</u> with your favorite leg, scissor or switch
legs and walkover out. The straighter the legs
and deeper the split, the better.

diving walkover

After taking several steps (the approach),
step hop, bringing straight arms backward and
low, then extend them forward as you step and
push off from one foot. Dive and walkover out.

back walkover

With the arms extended above the head
and the head <u>back</u> (eyes looking for the mat), <u>lift</u>
the forward extended leg (toes pointed) even
<u>before</u> the hands touch the mat. <u>Catch</u> the body's
weight on the hands, continue with the legs in
side split position to land on one foot. Learn it
with one hand when mastered. Spotter: to the
side of the acrobat, assist with one hand on the
back.

kangaroo
walkover

When taking the approach steps,
keep the arms <u>forward</u>, place hands on the mat
and <u>hop</u> 6-8 inches, keeping the legs split, then
walkover out.

front spotters

Off the mat, do a front walkover, <u>swing</u>
the forward foot backward then <u>step</u> on it,
walkover. In the same spot do several walkovers,
gaining momentum. Now you can join the
acrobats at the circus.

WALKOVER THEN GIANT STEP
BACK... YOU'RE THE BOSS...

front walkover
swing through

Walkover, then swing the forward foot
(before touching it) backward. Walkover, swing
the forward foot backward, walkover.

fancy walkover
combo

Begin a three-fancy-walkover series
by first doing one aeroplane walkover. Begin
another walkover, do the tap of the aeroplane, then
tap the feet (crossing them at the ankles), walkover
out. Do these two parts in the third walkover, then
split the legs, bending the lead leg to tap the head,
walkover out.

back walkover
special

Do a back walkover, bring feet together,
jump turn to face the other direction, land or slide
into a drop split. Bring the back leg to the front,
roll-up limber, front walkover.

Chapter 5

splits, stands, walks

D OING Splits on a regular basis is an excellent way to develop and maintain flexibility. This skill is much easier for youngsters than for adults, so start young! If practiced often, a large degree of flexibility can be maintained throughout the adult years. Then an unplanned fall may not result in injury.

As for any basic, be sure you do it properly. Correct form is more important than going clear down. Get a little closer to the floor each day.

In Headstands and Handstands, the body

should be as straight as possible. Both of these skills will transfer to gymnastic apparatus.

Losing and regaining body balance in a handstand describes what? Handwalking. The legs must <u>overbalance</u> in order to start the action. Handwalking tricks are FUN!

Do one or two steps at first. Soon, you'll be doing four or five, then ten. Try the many variations. Compete with friends.

SPLITS

side splits

With one leg forward and the other back, slide downward, catching the weight on the hands. When in a sitting position, the toes should be pointed, and the back leg turned under so that the knee is flat on the floor. What fun!

scissor circle splits

From a side split position, lean forward
onto the hands and stomach, bringing the legs
back. Cross what was the back leg over the other
one, swinging into the same side split again. Gain
momentum and spin like a top!

rolling circle split

With head down while holding the forward ankle, roll diagonally forward around in a circle, keeping in the split position.

handstand
drop split

Side split the legs while in a handstand, then start to come down. If the left leg is to lead forward into the split, lift the right arm. <u>Pulling in at the waist</u>, drop into the side split.

straddle split

With the legs apart, slide slowly down to a
sitting position with legs out to the sides.

See if you can lean far forward,
putting your arms out and chest on the floor. For
more challenge, hold the ankles.

STANDS

headstand
single leg lift

Start with your head and hands in a
triangle position. Keep your legs straight with feet
together on the mat, extend one leg at a time into
a headstand position. Spotter: stand beside acrobat
to catch the leg if needed.

headstand from
tuck position

Form a triangle with the head and hands.
Bend or flex the legs, keeping the body weight on
the hands and head (just above the hairline). Lift
the hips, keeping the legs bent, then straighten the
legs and hold the headstand. To me, this makes
more sense than resting the knees on the elbows
first. Balance is gained more easily.

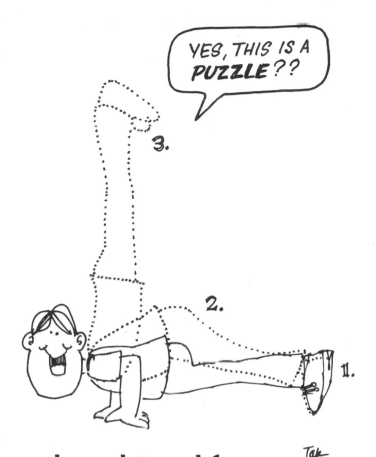

headstand from prone position

From a position on the stomach
a triangle formed with head and hands, <u>pull in</u> hard
with the abdominal muscles, bringing the hips <u>over</u>
the head with legs <u>straight</u>. Extend the legs
(straight) upward to a vertical headstand position.
Come down in exactly the same manner—very
controlled. You'll love to show this one to your
friends.

swedish fall

Lift one leg as you drop forward,
catching the weight on the hands, then flexing the
arms while turning the head to one side. Bring the
raised leg down, extend the arms as in push-up
position. Briefly drop the stomach, quickly bend the
legs and pull them between the arms to extend the
body in a back arch. Reach and turn to a front
support position, roll-out.

SWEDISH FALL...
WHO SAID IT WAS *EASY*?

elbow stand

Use a one-leg kick up, forearms positioned
with elbows directly under the shoulders, hands
spread, head back. Hold as long as you can, then
tuck the head and roll or come down the way you
went up. Try going from a headstand into an elbow
stand, one arm at a time. That's a real test of
balance and control!

HEY MOM, LOOK AT ME!!

scissor handstand

Kick up with one leg then the other,
coming down on the first leg. The head is back
towards the upper back, and the hands (fingers
spread) are directly under the shoulders. This is the
lead-up used to strengthen the arms and gain in
body control prior to handstands.

vertical handstand

After placing the hands 10-12 inches
from the wall, kick up into a handstand (one leg at
a time). Keep as straight as possible, head back. To
learn to hold it, bend one leg and tap the wall a
few times, gaining balance. When ready straighten
the leg—hold it. Be sure to use a mat. Practice!

headstand to handstand

In a headstand position, bend the legs,
then <u>shoot</u> them upward, pressing on the hands,
into a handstand. Split the legs, walk out. This is a
challenge in timing and coordination. It also
strengthens the arms.

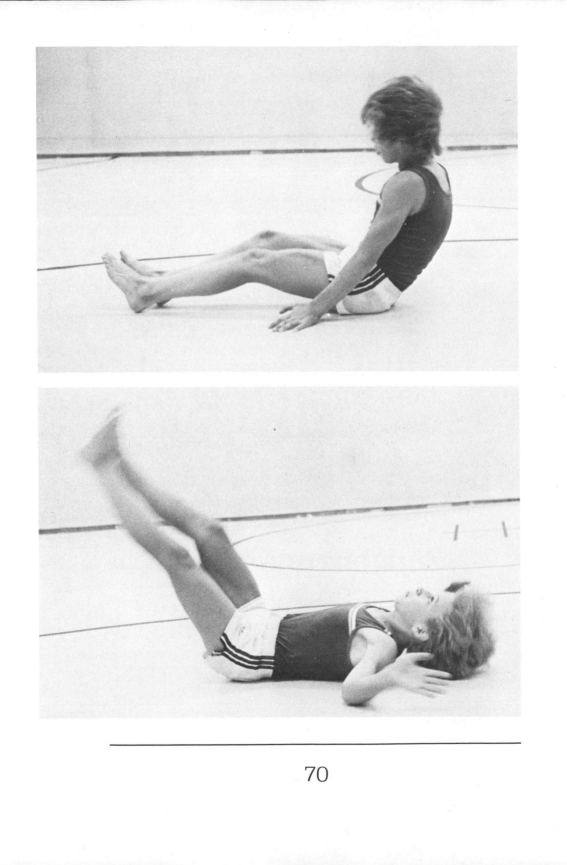

back extension

Begin as in a pike back roll, push on the hands, then shoot the legs <u>diagonally</u> forward (due to the momentum). From the handstand, come down with the feet together in pike position or snap down flexing the legs. You may want to split the legs and walk out. Spotter: from this side, assist by holding the legs above the knee in the headstand position.

WALKS

Handwalking—Walking on the hands is a losing and regaining of the balance with each step. OVERBALANCE the legs to start forward movement.

Handwalk Ear Touch—Handwalk with legs together, <u>touch</u> the ear with the hand, then repeat it on the other side, etc., as you take each step.

Scissor Handwalking—After walking with legs in a side split position, begin to <u>switch</u> legs with each step.

Handstand Circle Walkover—Kick into a side split handstand, lift one hand, moving it toward yourself and around 180 degrees, walkover out.

Neon Sign—In a side split handstand, tap one leg with the other, split, tap head with forward foot, split etc., as you handwalk.

Carol's Pro Special

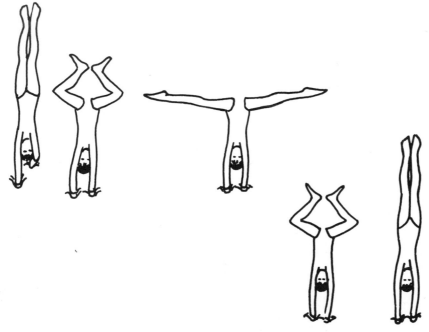

Handstand, flex, straddle split, flex, handstand

Fast circle hand walk, drop split

From the drop split, kick to a split handstand, walkover.

Chapter 6

springs

S PRINGS are <u>fun</u>!
They're <u>exciting</u>! It's
like "flying" through space for a short time. Of
course, the first few springs are slow and
mechanical. Time spent here will pay off later.
Your springs will be straight and correct. Having
been the Women's Gymnastic Coach at Colorado
State University, I can tell you that trying to
correct basics after they have become firmly
fixed habits is frustrating and only partially
successful. So practice well.

You will be pleasantly surprised when you
put two headsprings together—then three.

Momentum builds and you will go zipping across the mats like you had four "C" batteries in your back! For you older youngsters, pretend your brother is after you, and "go like sixty!"

Headspring—From a triangular position with the head and hands, legs piked and parallel to the floor, <u>overbalance</u> the hips, <u>push</u> on the hands and land in a squat. When perfected learn to <u>arch</u>. Spotter: one hand under upper arm, one on wrist.

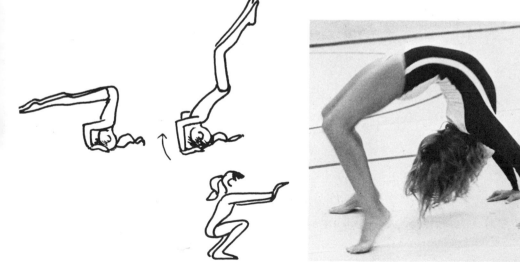

Kip or Nip-Up—While supported on the hands and upper back with legs in pike position, drop the hips somewhat then throw the legs forward and flex while pushing off with the hands. Land as if sitting in a chair when learning, then later arch and walk out like a walkover. Spotter: lift with hands under upper arm.

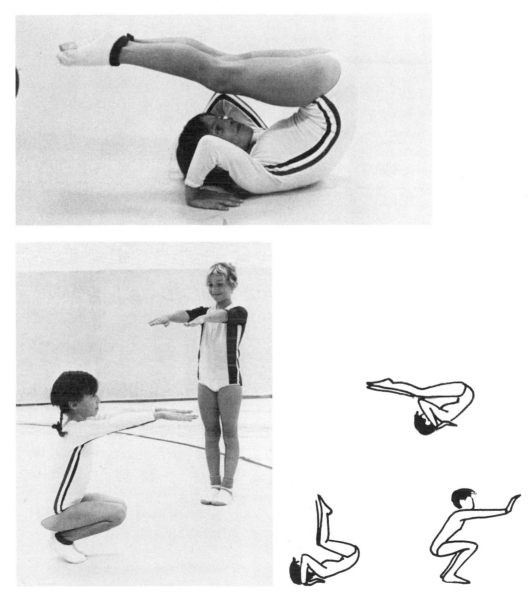

Front Handspring—With a one-foot take-off, bring the feet together when vertical. <u>Push</u> with the hands, landing in a squat position, arms forward. When mastered, try the <u>arched</u> position, landing vertically. Spotter: put one hand on the back.

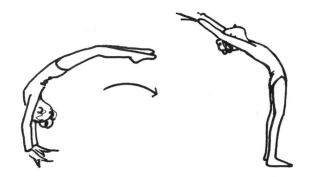

mule kicks

In a handstand, bend the legs, then whip or snap them down, <u>pushing</u> off hard with the hands, <u>flexing</u> or bending the legs. Leap onto the hands. They should not touch the floor until the feet have left it, and when the hands push off, the feet must not touch the floor until the hands have left. Repeat in rhythm. This is great preparation for other skills to come.

index